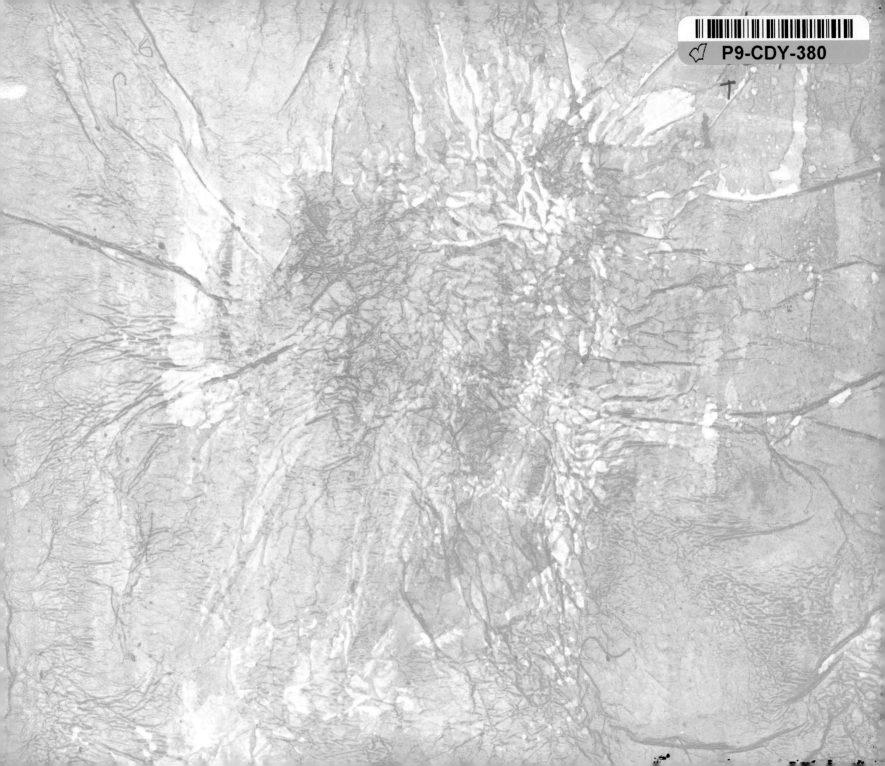

HENRY Z. WALCK, INCORPORATED   NEW YORK

A BOY ONCE LIVED IN NAZARETH

BY FLORENCE M. TAYLOR

ILLUSTRATED BY LEN EBERT

Newark United Methodist Church
Newark, Delaware

Long ago and far away
a boy once lived
in Nazareth.

His home was like the others
along the village street,
one single room,
with stairs outside
to the flat roof
protected by a parapet.
His father was the village carpenter.
His shop stood close
beside his home,
and to the boy it was
a fascinating place.

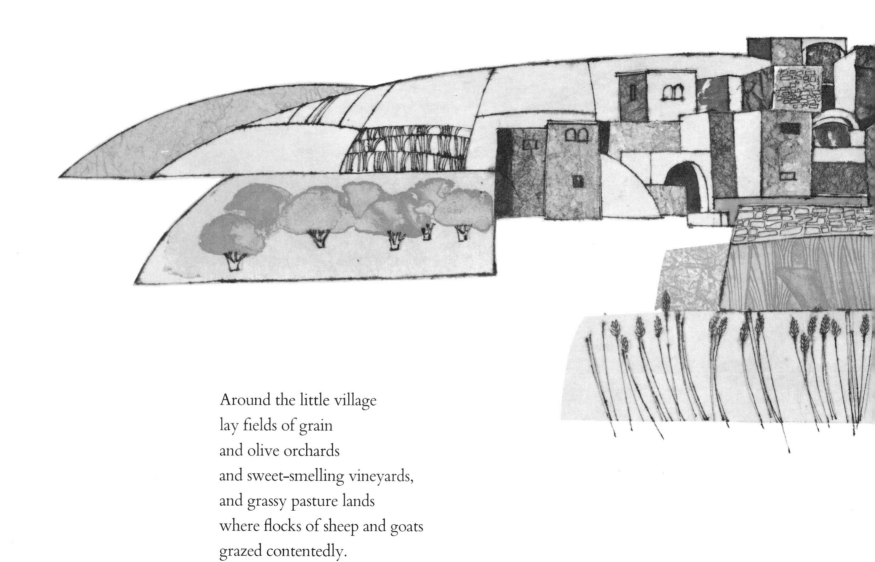

Around the little village
lay fields of grain
and olive orchards
and sweet-smelling vineyards,
and grassy pasture lands
where flocks of sheep and goats
grazed contentedly.

The boy liked to wake up
in the early morning
and hear the birds
call softly from the trees;
he used to slip out
of the crowded little house
into the dusty street.

He liked to run
on swift, brown feet
along the narrow roadway
out to the open hills;
to climb and climb
and feel the warmth of sun,
the cooling breeze,
the dew-wet grass
against his feet.

He liked to lie full length
among the fragrant flowers
of the field
and let the quiet hillside
fill his mind
with wonderings.

The boy was the oldest brother
in the home,
often charged with the care
of younger children.
He was a happy playmate;
the children welcomed him with joy
to share their play.

Newark United Methodist Church
Newark, Delaware

He liked to work with tools
keen-edged and shining,
to use the saw and plane,
to smell the clean, sweet wood
and shape it skillfully
to many uses.

He often found his way
down to the marketplace
and watched the merchants
in their stalls,
the crowding people.
He liked the noise,
the busy, changing scene,
the coming of the caravans,
the tales that strangers told
of distant places,
unfamiliar customs.

With other village lads
he went to school.
The schoolhouse was the synagogue;
the rabbi taught the boys.
The books were ancient scrolls,
cloth-wrapped and very precious,
kept in the Ark
and handled reverently
with gentle hands.

In them was written
all the history
of the boy's people—
the well-known stories
of heroes long since gone,
the songs of joy and sorrow,
the binding laws
by which the people lived.

All these the boy
learned in the synagogue school
and stored up in his heart.

Sometimes on quiet summer days
the boy sought out
the shepherds with their flocks
in grassy meadows
far beyond the town.

He shared their simple lunch
of bread and cheese
and sweet dried dates and figs,
and listened to their talk
of birth and life and death.

At harvest time
he shared the village toil.
He helped to tie the ripened grain
in sheaves.
He knew the harvest law
that bade the reapers
leave grain still standing
in the corners of the field,
for those who had
no grain fields of their own.

He watched the donkey
treading round and round
on the heaped grain
to separate the kernels
from the chaff.
He watched the threshers
toss the grain on high
to let the strong wind
blow away the chaff
and leave the heavy kernels.

The boy helped gather up
the fallen olives,
when the men
beat the laden branches
to send the dark fruit
tumbling down like rain.
He knew the harvest law
that no tree should be
beaten twice—
some olives must be left
for those
who owned no olive trees.

He helped the workers
in the vineyards
pile on flat baskets
the heavy purple clusters
of ripe grapes,
leaving some still on the vines
for those in need.
He ate his fill
of the sweet, juicy fruit.

He liked the peaceful hours
when work was done;
when on the roof
the family sat together
in quiet fellowship
beneath the brilliant stars;
or walked with friends
and neighbors
along the narrow street,
to offer in the synagogue
their thanks and praise to God.

The boy played and worked
and studied,
went busily about
his daily tasks
with clear, all-seeing eyes,
with heart responsive
to each person's need;
each act a token
of the deep, out-reaching love
that filled his heart;
each act of every busy day
an offering of himself
to God.

A boy once lived
in Nazareth.
His name was Jesus.

And Jesus increased in wisdom and stature,
and in favor with God and man.

Luke 2:52